I, Vivaldi

Written by Janice Shefelman

Illustrated by Tom Shefelman

Eerdmans Books for Young Readers

Grand Rapids, Michigan ❖ Cambridge, U.K.

Venice
1678

On the day that I, Antonio Lucio Vivaldi, was born, there was an earthquake. My mama heard a rumble from under the ground. Church bells were ringing all over town.

My papa ran up the stairs. "Camilla, we have to get out of the house!"

"But Giovanni," Mama cried, "the baby is coming. You must go for the midwife!"

Papa hurried out and fetched Madama Margarita. By then the earth had stopped shaking, but no one knew when it might start again.

Before long I arrived, gasping for breath.

"Alas, I am afraid he has trouble breathing," said the midwife. "We must baptize him immediately."

Madama Margarita summoned my papa. Then she recited the holy words and dribbled water over my head.

"Dear Mary, Mother of God," said Mama, "if my firstborn child is spared, I swear, sure as the tide comes in and goes out, he will become a priest."

I took a breath and let out a loud cry.

"Bravo!" said Papa. "My son is a fighter."

So I survived, but Mama's vow would cause much trouble.

Every day I awoke to the sound of the church bells ringing outside my window. And soon afterward, to the singing of Papa's violin.

One morning I crept downstairs to his studio. He was so busy playing his violin that he did not notice me. I watched him and pretended to play my own violin.

"Papa, look!"

"Ah, Antonio, my little musician. Shall we play a duet?"

When I was four, Papa bought a small violin for me.

Mama did not like the idea. "He is not going to be a musician, so he does not need a violin."

"Camilla, this violin gives Antonio something to do, since he can't run and play with other boys."

That was true. Running made my chest feel tight.

Mama sighed and left the room.

"So, we shall begin your lessons!" Papa took up his violin. "First we tune." He pulled his bow across a string. "That is the note we call 'A.' Now you try it."

I raised my bow.

"You must draw the bow lightly across the strings, Antonio, as if your hand were held by invisible wings."

I drew my bow across the A string. Papa turned the A peg until we sounded alike. When my violin was tuned we played together — two strokes on each string. It was like breathing in and out, only easier.

"You learn quickly, my son."

From then on Papa gave me lessons twice a week, and I practiced every day.

The neighborhood boys often
played in the courtyard. Once, I tried
to join them, but my chest felt tight
when I chased after the ball.

Mama called me back inside.
"How many times must I tell you,
Antonio? God never meant you to
run." She smiled and held my
face in her hands. "You barely
survived your first day.
That's why I vowed you
would become a priest."

"God meant me to
be a violinist, Mama,
not a priest."

Mama made the sign
of the cross. "Forgive
him, God. He does not
know what he is saying."

I knew exactly what I was saying, but
Mama did not want to hear it. So I stomped
upstairs and played a fast piece that expressed
the anger in my heart.

One morning as Papa was leaving for rehearsal, he said, "Antonio, get your violin and come with me."

"Giovanni, no!" Mama said.

"My dear, Antonio is seven years old. He needs to see what I do."

"He can see without his violin."

Papa took her hand and kissed it. "Please, Camilla, allow me a little fatherly pride."

I picked up my violin and followed him out the door.

We boarded a gondola for the Piazza San Marco. Everywhere there was music. People played instruments and sang at their windows, on the bridges, and on boats. My heart sang too.

As we walked across the piazza, I stared at the Church of San Marco. My eyes could not get enough of the murals, made of millions of colorful stones, or the golden horses standing high above the entrance.

While Papa rehearsed, I tapped my foot to the music, hoping he would ask me to play.

At last Papa spoke to the conductor. "Maestro, what would you think of letting my Antonio join us for the next one?"

"Yes, of course," he said. "Come, my boy."

I took out my violin and stood beside Papa. The maestro raised his hands, and we were off! My fingers galloped about on the strings. I forgot everything but the music.

When we finished, the maestro turned to my papa. "Giovanni, you have a most talented son."

Then and there I made a vow that music would be my life.

The years passed, and before long I turned fifteen.

One evening Mama announced, "Antonio, it is time to begin your studies for the priesthood."

"But I want to be a musician like Papa." I glanced at my brother. "Perhaps Tomaso could become a priest instead."

Papa sighed. "No, it was *you* that she promised. You owe your life to that vow."

"I don't care. I've made my own vow."

Mama stood up. "Antonio, you will become a priest!"

"Then I will die!"

There was a breathless silence.

Papa looked me in the eye. "You will keep your mother's vow." He turned to Mama. "But I understand the boy. Perhaps if he gave up the violin he *would* die."

Mama's eyes softened. "Very well, Antonio, but your studies come first."

So I began my studies, but they did not come first. Music did. I played the violin, composed music, and three more years passed.

"Why is it taking so long for you to become a priest?" Mama asked.

"Mama, you know God never meant me to run."

"Do not mock me, Antonio. You may be a man, but I am still your mother."

Finally I was ordained, and people began calling me the Red
Priest for the color of my hair. Red Violinist would be better.

One day, I stopped beside a canal. I listened to the water lapping against the walls of houses and a nightingale singing from its cage. I watched gondoliers rowing by. The sounds and rhythms were like music.

"Ah, the Red Priest," a gondolier called from his boat. "May I take you home?"

"Yes, please. My head is filled with music, and I can write it down as we go." I stepped into his gondola, sat back, and began to turn the sounds and rhythms into musical notes. If only I could do nothing but make music. There was so little time!

Even so, my fame as a violinist grew. Count Contarini invited
me to his palace to perform some new music I had written. I
closed my eyes and put all my longing into it. Suddenly I heard
a sigh. It was the countess. She had swooned in delight. Once
again I vowed to make music my whole life. But how?

Here I must confess something that I never admitted in public. Once, during Mass, music came flooding into my head. I could not think of the words I was saying. And I could hardly breathe for the tightness in my chest.

So I rushed out of the service to write down the notes before I forgot them.

I dipped the quill in the ink well, and the notes flew across the page. I could scarcely write fast enough, but now I could breathe again.

When I was finished, I hurried back to the service. It was over! And there stood the bishop.

"How dare you leave during Mass!" he hissed. "The cardinal will hear about this."

"Then tell him, Your Excellency, that I do not wish to say Mass again. I wish to make music."

The bishop stared at me as if I had gone mad. Indeed, I felt so gloriously mad that I turned and ran out of the church.

The cardinal *did* hear about me. "You have certainly behaved badly, Antonio," he said.

"Your Eminence, on bended knee I most humbly beg your gracious self to pardon this sickly, mad creature that I am." (Such is the way one must speak to cardinals.)

He studied me for a moment. "It is true that you musicians are quite mad. And that being so, I shall grant your wish. Instead of saying Mass, you will teach violin to orphan girls."

I bowed in thanks. Now music could be my whole life!

Not only did I teach violin, I also conducted the orchestra and wrote music for the poor, fortunate girls. Poor because most were abandoned. Fortunate because those who had a talent for music could study it.

They had no last names, so each one was given the name of the instrument she played, such as Catarina of the Viola or Bettina of the Bassoon.

How eager they were to play my music! At every rehearsal they would ask for something new. So I composed more and more music for them.

Zephyr

Notus

The girls inspired me to try a new kind of
composition that makes musical pictures. I called it
The Four Seasons. After we played the music together
for the first time, they all began talking at once.

Boreas

Eureus

"Maestro," said Bianca, "I can hear birds singing in my violin."
"And I make the thunder rumble with my cello," Luciana said.
"And we make the dog bark," said Catarina of the Viola.
"So it is fitting," I said, "that I play the cuckoo."
They all laughed.

On Sundays and holidays, we gave concerts in the
chapel. Strange as it may sound, those orphan girls became
the finest musicians in Italy. People came from all over Europe
to hear us and get a peek at the girls. Papa and Mama always came.

And sometimes kings did, too. Once, King Frederick of Denmark
attended our concert. The girls became quite nervous beforehand.

"Just play from your heart, and it will touch his," I told them.

We played a violin sonata, music I had composed especially for him. When we
were finished, everyone waited for the king to respond.

He began to cough and scrape his feet on the floor to show his pleasure, for
applause was not permitted in the chapel. Some men in the audience blew their
noses into lace handkerchiefs. Mama and other women tapped fans on the arms
of their chairs.

After the concert, Papa looked proud and Mama was beaming.

"Antonio, you are not the kind of priest I thought you would be," she said.
"But you are surely making music for God."

Fact & Fiction

You probably want to know what is fact and what is fiction. In the Venice of Antonio Vivaldi's day there were strict laws of behavior, so people kept their lives private to avoid trouble. Thus Antonio remains a shadowy figure. I wanted to shine some light on him by using facts to imagine fiction.

Here are the facts: He was born on the day of an earthquake and baptized by the midwife, Madama Margarita, because he had trouble breathing and they thought he might die. Later he was officially baptized in the Church of San Giovanni.

When Antonio was a boy, his father taught him to play the violin and took him along to rehearsals. Antonio became known for his violin playing and, in time, for his compositions. After he was ordained, people began to call him the Red Priest. But soon he stopped saying Mass to teach at the Pietà, an orphanage for girls, although the reasons are not certain.

There was a rumor that he left the altar during Mass one day to write down music. Antonio denied it, saying he left because of the tightness in his chest. Perhaps it was a little of both. He had a way of saying whatever was necessary to get what he wanted. But in his music Antonio Vivaldi said what was in his heart.

People in Venice had an appetite for new music, and eventually Vivaldi's lost favor. In 1740 he left Venice and traveled to Vienna, where he died in 1741, poor and forgotten.

Today *The Four Seasons* is one of the most popular pieces of classical music in the world. My favorite recording is by the Italian chamber orchestra, *Il Giardino Armonico* (The Harmonious Garden).

Antonio composed hundreds of other beautiful pieces, including church music and operas. Once again we can feel the energy and longing that he turned into music.

—J. S.

Glossary

cardinal:	high official in the Catholic Church
gondola:	(GON-doh-lah) water taxi
gondolier:	(gon-doh-LEER) person who rows a gondola
maestro:	title given to a composer or conductor of music
Mass:	religious service in the Catholic Church
midwife:	woman who helps in the birth of a baby
ordained:	made a priest
piazza:	(pee-AHT-zah) Italian word meaning open public square

Listen & Play

You may enjoy listening to *The Compleat Four Seasons* conducted by Arnie Roth and narrated by Patrick Stewart on an American Gramaphone compact disc (AGCD801). Or you can play the beginning of "Spring" yourself, using the music printed below. If you listen with your heart as well as your ears, you can share Antonio's feelings across hundreds of years.

Spring

VIOLIN I   from "The Four Seasons"   Antonio Vivaldi
                                                                                          Arr. by Richard Meyer

For Tom
my one and only illustrator
— *J. S.*

For Janice
my partner in life and art
— *T. S.*

Text © Janice Shefelman
Illustrations © Tom Shefelman

Published in 2008 by Eerdmans Books for Young Readers
an imprint of Wm. B. Eerdmans Publishing Co.

All rights reserved

Wm. B. Eerdmans Publishing Co.
2140 Oak Industrial Dr. NE, Grand Rapids, Michigan 49505
P.O. Box 163, Cambridge CB3 9PU U.K.

www.eerdmans.com/youngreaders

Manufactured in China

08 09 10 11 12 13 14   8 7 6 5 4 3 2 1

Library of Congress Cataloging-in-Publication Data
Shefelman, Janice Jordan, 1930-
I, Vivaldi / written by Janice Shefelman ; illustrated by Tom Shefelman.
    p. cm.
ISBN 978-0-8028-5318-9 (alk. paper)
Vivaldi, Antonio, 1678-1741--Juvenile literature.
2. Composers—Italy—Biography—Juvenile literature.
I. Shefelman, Tom, ill. II. Title.
 ML3930.V58S5 2007
 780.92--dc22
 [B]   2006020120

Display type set in Vivaldi
Text type set in Venetian 301
Illustrations created using ink line and watercolor

Music on the endpapers:
"Winter" from *The Four Seasons*, Antonio Vivaldi
Published by Le Cene, Amsterdam, 1725
© Alamire Music Publishers
Used with their kind permission
www.alamire.com

Music for Listen & Play:
"Spring" from *The Four Seasons*, Antonio Vivaldi
Arranged by Richard Meyer
© MCMXCIX by Highland Etling
A Division of Alfred Publishing Co., Inc.
All Rights Reserved
Used by Permission of Alfred Publishing Co., Inc.